Japanese Gardens of the Modern Era

Photographs by HARUZO OHASHI

Each photo caption is described as follows :
Roka Sensui-so Water Basin Taisho Era Shiga
Title   Item   Time   Place

Published by Graphic-sha Publishing Co., Ltd.
1-9-12 Kudankita, Chiyoda-ku, Tokyo, Japan.

Distributors:
UNITED STATES: Kodansha International/USA, Ltd.,
through Harper & Row, Publishers, Inc., 10 East 53rd
Street, New York, N.Y. 10022. SOUTH AMERICA: Harper
& Row, Publishers, Inc., International Department.
CANADA: Fitzhenry & Whiteside Ltd., 195 Allstate Parkway,
Markham, Ontario L3R 4T8. MEXICO AND CENTRAL
AMERICA: HARLA S.A. de C.V., Apartado 30-546,
Mexico 4, D.F. BRITISH ISLES: International Book
Distributors Ltd., 66 Wood Lane End, Hemel Hempstead,
Herts HP2 4RG England. EUROPEAN CONTINENT:
Proost & Brandt Distribution, 61 Strijkviertel, 3454 PK DE
MEERN, The Netherlands. Australia and New Zealand:
Bookwise International, 1 Jeanes Street, Beverley, South
Australia 5007. THE FAR EAST: Japan Publications
Trading Co., 1-2-1, Sarugaku-cho, Chiyoda-ku, Tokyo 101.

First Printing: September 1987
ISBN 0-87040-743-0

Printed in Japan

Japanese Gardens of the Modern Era

Contents

SAISEI'S GARDENING

ASAKO MUROO (Author)

As lons as I can remember over the past 30 years I have grown up gazing at the gardens planted by my father, Saisei. Without belonging to any school of thought or any teaching of Japanese gardens for that matter, he called the gardens he landscaped Saisei-style gardens. He had the same passion for gardens as for his novels and always held these passions close to his heart.

He first started to putter around in the garden after our family had returned to our hometown, Kanazawa, one month after I was born following the Great Kanto Earthquake. We lived in a rented house siutated in front of the river in Kawagishi-machi at the foot of Sakurabashi Bridge of Saigawa River. We lived there till the summer of 1916. Just 5 years ago that house was rebuilt. The next-door neighbor, Mr. Izumi, was the landlord and I remeber the old grandmother Izumi telling me stories as a child. The branches of the pine tree hung just perfectly over the wooden gate. On the right side of the house there was a garden bordered with a board fence, over which Mr. Izumi's house stood. One day my father told Mr. Izumi that he would like to plant a garden on the south side and asked if it was all right. Dumbfound, Mr. Izumi gave his consent.

There was the famous garden, Kenrokuen Garden, in Kanazawa as well as many gardens that could be privately owned. Attractive miniature gardens could be found at inns and restaurants.

Mr. Izumi probably thought why on the south side. The next day the gardener came, removed all the trees and bushes, and piled them in a corner of the garden. Then, he brought in some hemp palms and Japanese banana plants. The appearance of the garden had undergone a complete metamorphosis. Only the apricot tree was left standing as it was. Until the snow came, the rustling sound of the banana plant leaves swaying in the wind did not fit in with the natural landscape of Kanazawa. At that time my father wrote the poem, "The Rubber Tree." I never knew why it caught his fancy even temporarily.

He rented the temple grounds of the Tentokuin Temple in Kanazawa in 1928 and built a one-room 4.5 tatami mat hut with a garden. When a large mansion and garden was up for sale, he bought a tsukubai, stone washbasin, Oribe lanterns, stepping stones as well as two tawara bags of Okaayame. I learned of this from the novel, "The Sale of Boteki-an," and his journal.

Even when we lived in a rented house in Tokyo, we went to Kanazawa in a sleeping car and stayed for

3—4 days. A neighborhood woman would prepare our meals for us. I faintly remember that garden. There was a small stream flowing in the middle of it while a wide street flanked the main gate in front. The back wooden door faced a narrow street running along the fields. I was about 5 years old then. I met the son of the gardener who was in charge of the garden. My father had wanted to bring in some Dutch rushes. There were very few Dutch rushes in the snow country and it was extremely difficult to find them.

When we built our house in Tokyo, we brought almost different kinds of lanterns and stones from the Kanazawa garden. Within a lifetime Saisei's garden took on many forms and shapes. The family's life occupied the center of his mind. On one side of that there was his work and on the other side there was his garden. Tied to both was his spiritual soul that always ran parallel like a river. For instance, after finishing a big work such as a long novel he would turn to the garden and start to remodel it as a way to work off the left-over energy or as a way to soothe the sould fatigued from work.

Someone remarked to my father that since he loved gardens so much he should go and see the famous gardens in Kyoto but my father replied, "If I went to Kyoto I would soon imitate them. So it is better that I don't."

Nevertheless, he did visit Kyoto in 1936 and paid pilgrimage to the temples of Kotoin, Saihoji, Daitokuji and others, while he wrote the book "Kyoraku Nikki."

I wonder what inspired my father's passion for gardening. I think it was most probably due to the constant influence of Kenrokuen Garden in his childhood days. Looking at it from day to day became the underlying foundation. Someday I want to stroll in Kenrokuen Garden and take in every tree and shrub as I compare them to the memory of my father's garden. Then I would like to write a book on his life, work and gardening.

Editorial Director: **Kakuzo Akahira**

Design: **Hiroto Kumagai**

1 *Hiyoshi Shrine Iwakura Ancient Times Shiga*

2 *Achi Shrine Iwakura (Tsurushima Stone Grouping) Ancient Times Okayama*

3 *Former Oyaku-en Garden of Mr. Nanbu's The Central Part of Chitei Edo Era Iwate*

4 *Former Yubi-kan A Complete View Edo Era Miyagi*

5 *Mr. Nishida's Gyokusen-en Garden Rock Island Edo Era Ishikawa*

6 *Mr. Izome's Tennenzugaku-tei A Complete View of the Study Room Edo Era Shiga*

7 *Mantokuji A Complete View Edo Era Fukui*

8 *Former Private Garden of Mr. Sakai's Rock Island Edo Era Yamagata*

9 *Takidanji The Central Part of Chitei Edo Era Fukui*

10 *Former Umenoki Honjin* *A Complete View Edo Era Shiga*

11 *Former Private Garden of Mr. Yasuda's Shinshu-en Sawawatari Stone Grouping Edo Era Tokyo*

12 *Mr. Ozaki's Private Residence A Complete View Edo Era Tottori*

13 *Mr. Kakei's Private Residence Chitei Viewed from the Study Room Edo Era Hiroshima*

14 *Manganji Stone Bridge in Chitei Edo Era Kumamoto*

15 *Mr. Noborizaka's Private Residence The Central part of Karesansui Edo Era Iwate*

16 *Mr. Ayugai's En-un-kan The Central Part of Chitei Edo Era Miyagi*

17 *Nyoshi-tei Sanzon Stone Grouping Edo Era Akita*

18 *Homma Museum A Complete View Edo Era Yamagata*

19 *Ryuunji Three-step Nagaretaki Stone Grouping Edo Era Niigata*

20 *Gonenji Karetaki Stone Grouping Edo Era Hyogo*

21 *Yosui-en A Complete View Edo Era Wakayama*

22 *Unkiji A Complete View Edo Era Shimane*

23 *Mr. Shoji's Private Residence A Complete View Edo Era Tottori*

24 *Mr. Sakurai's Private Residence Nagaretaki Stone Grouping Edo Era Shimane*

25 *Tensha-en A Complete View Edo Era Ehime*

26 *Mr. Naotada Sata's Private Residence Enzan Stone Grouping Edo Era Kagoshima*

27 *Enyuji Shudan (Mass) Stone Grouping Edo Era Nagasaki*

28 *Mr. Ie's Private Residence Stone Bridge of Chitei Meiji Era Okinawa*

29 *Former Zuiraku-en Garden of the Tsushima's A Complete View Meiji Era Aomori*

30 *Former Kasai-so Villa The Central Part of Karesansui Meiji Era Iwate*

31 *Mr. Kon's Private Residence A Complete-View Meiji Era Iwate*

32 *Mr. Koyama's Kiyo-tei A Complete View Meiji Era Yamagata*

33 *Hoppo Bunka Museum A Complete View Meiji Era Niigata*

34 *Mr. Senke's Private Residence A Complete View Meiji Era Shimane*

35 *Former Sakyoya Mr. Matsuura's Private Residence The Central Part of Chitei Meiji Era Shiga*

36 *Murin-an Stream in the Central Part of the Garden Meiji Era Kyoto*

37 *Isui-en Sawawatari Stepping Stones Meiji Era Nara*

38 *Isui-en* The Snowy *Chitei Meiji Era Nara*

39 *Mr. Tachibana's Shoto-en Garden The Central Part of Chitei Meiji Era Fukuoka*

40 *Mr. Furukawa's Private Residence A Complete View of Karikomi* *Taisho Era Tokyo*

41 *Mr. Hashimoto's Hakusha-sonso Stone Buddhist Images in a Bamboo Forest Taisho Era Kyoto*

42 *Mr. Hashimoto's Hakusha-sonso Seven-story Pagoda Taisho Era Kyoto*

43 *Mr. Hashimoto's Hakusha-sonso Hokyoin Pagoda Taisho Era Kyoto*

44 *Mr. Hashimoto's Hakusha-sonso Kunisaki Sekido Taisho Era Kyoto*

45 *Mr. Hashimoto's Hakusha-sonso Stone Buddhist Relief Taisho Era Kyoto*

46 *Sankei-en A Complete View Taisho Era Kanagawa*

47 *Sankei-en Shunsoro Taisho Era Kanagawa*

48 *Sankei-en Shunsoro Tsukubai Taisho Era Kanagawa*

49 *Roka Sensui-so Flagstones Taisho Era Shiga*

50 *Roka Sensui-so Lantern Taisho Era Shiga*

51 *Roka Sensui-so Water Basin Taisho Era Shiga*

52 *Heian Shrine Sawawatari Stepping Stones Taisho Era Kyoto*

53 *Heian Shrine Pavilion over a Pond Taisho Era Kyoto*

54 *Onzan-so Garden Path and Chitei Taisho Era Wakayama*

55 *Komyozen-in Moss Present Age Kyoto*

56 *Mr. Shigemori's Private Residence Ajiromon Present Age Kyoto*

57 *Mr. Shigemori's Private Residence Igetamon Present Age Kyoto*

58 *Mr. Shigemori's Private Residence Seikaihamon Present Age Kyoto*

59 *Mr. Shigemori's Private Residence Uzumakimon Present Age Kyoto*

60 *Mr. Shigemori's Private Residence Ajiromon Variation Present Age Kyoto*

61 *Mr. Shigemori's Private Residence Kyokusenmon Present Age Kyoto*

62 *Matsuo Taisha Iwakura (Egoishi Stone Grouping) Present Age Kyoto*

63 *Tofukuji The Central Part of Karesansui Present Age Kyoto*

64 *Tofukuji A Partial View of Karesansui Present Age Kyoto*

65 *Tofukuji A Complete View Present Age Kyoto*

66 *Shokakuji A Complete View Present Age Hyogo*

67 *Kozenji A Complete View Present Age Nagano*

68 *Shogunzuka Around the Stone Bridge Present Age Kyoto*

69 *Adachi Art Museum The Central Part of Karesansui Present Age Shimane*

70 *Komine Shrine Flagstones Present Age Tochigi*

71 *Komine Shrine Nagaretaki Stone Grouping Present Age Tochigi*

72 *Ryugen-in A Complete View of the East Garden Present Age Kyoto*

73 *Mr. Morita's Private Residence A View from a Room Present Age Chiba*

74 *Mr. Yano's Private Residence A View from the Study Room Present Age Tokushima*

75 *Hotel Koyokan The Central Part of Chitei Present Age Iwate*

76 *Hotel Hanamaki Nagaretaki Stone Grouping Present Age Iwate*

77 Hotel Hanamaki Otsu-gaki Variation Present Age Iwate

78 *Kifune-cho Chasen-gaki Present Age Kyoto*

79 *Tokoen Hotel Daitokuji-gaki Present Age Tottori*

80 *Kifune-cho Katsura-gaki Variation Present Age Kyoto*

81 *Hanamaki Hot Spring Sosaku-gaki Present Age Iwate*

82 *Mr. Idemitsu's Private Residence The Middle Gate of Choseki-an Present Age Tokyo*

83 *Mr. Idemitsu's Private Residence Yakuishi at the Middle Gate of Choseki-an Present Age Tokyo*

84 *Mr. Okazaki's Private Residence Seisui-an Nakakuguri (Wicket Gate) Present Age Fukuoka*

85 *Mr. Okazaki's Private Residence Seisui-an Tsukubai Present Age Fukuoka*

86 *Hakone Art Museum Around the Sangetsu-an Present Age Kanagawa*

87 *Hakone Art Museum The Middle Gate of Sangetsu-an Present Age Kanagawa* 88 *Hakone Art Museum Sangetsu-an Machiai Present Age Kanagawa*

89 *Tea Ceremony Association (Dainihon Chado Gakkai) Santoku-an Nijiriguchi Present Age Tokyo*

90 *Tea Ceremony Association (Dainihon Chado Gakkai) Santoku-an Machiai Present Age Tokyo*

91 *Tea Ceremony Association (Dainihon Chado Gakkai) Santoku-an Chiriana Present Age Tokyo*

92 *Tea Ceremony Association (Dainihon Chado Gakkai) The Well of Santoku-an Present Age Tokyo*

1 Hiyoshi Shrine, "A Complete View of Iwakura", Ancient Times (Shiga)

A very old Shrine whose name is found in "Kojiki" ("Records of Ancient Matters"). It is the head shrine of 3,800 Sanno Shrines throughout the country. This is a site for religious rites, with God descending upon the great rock to dwell within it. I feel both the rock seat on the hilltop and the boulder on the flat ground might be the origins of the Japanese garden.
LINHOF KARDAN FUJINON 210mm F5.6 f22 1/2 EPR

2 Achi Shrine, "Iwakura (Tsurushima Stone Grouping)", Ancient Times (Okayama)

Many shrines all over the country house stones as objects of worship. The impulse to erect, lay or set stones (to make a stone grouping) originates with an instinctive love of stones. Ancient people's attachment to stones was sublimated into worship as a way to treasure and enshrine stones. It has been passed down to the present day.
LINHOF KARDAN FUJINON 210mm F5.6 f22 1/2 EPR

3 Former Oyaku-en Garden of Mr. Nanbu's, "The Central Part of Chitei", Edo Era (Iwate)

Ponds and lakes play a central role in most of the gardens of feudal lords. It was a clever way to maintain the garden by growing medical herbs there for distribution to people in the fief. The green reflected on the surface of the crisp water is serenely beautiful. Manay people choose this place for their strolls.
LINHOF SYMMAR 150mm F5.6 f16 1/4 EPR

4 Former Yubi-kan, "A Complete View", Edo Era, (Miyagi)

Toshichika Date, the third generation master, had Yubi-kan built in 1691 as a school to educate sons of his retainers. In the garden made by Dokan Shimizu, a votary of the tea cult in Sendai, four islands are arranged in a pond 500m round, with a castle on the hill as the background. The grove of Japanese red pine trees is particularly beautiful.
SINAR P SYMMAR 150mm F5.6 f11 1/8 EPR

5 Mr. Nishida's Gyokusen-en, "Garden Rock Island", Edo Era (Ishikawa)

The garden is located very close to the Kenrokuen, the primary sight-seeing spot in Kanazawa City. The pond area was designed to make use of the hillside configuration of the ground and the upper area, with its tearoom; Reisetsu-tei presents a typical stroll garden. In this photo, the plants that thrive on the rock island in the pond give focus to the vast garden.
LINHOF KARDAN SYMMAR 150mm F5.6 f22 1/4 EPR

6 Mr. Izome's Tennenzugaku-tei, "A complete View of the Study Room", Edo Era (Shiga)

The Izomes led the Katada armed forces for generations and owned the navigation rights to Lake Biwa. Many of the descendants of the family were known as men of refined tastes who associated with such masters of chanoyu as Yuan Kitamura and Yoken Fujimura. The place was frequented by men of letters and artists. Both the Shoin building and the garden of the ceremonial teahouse display beauty of perfection, and still attract admirers.
LINHOF NIKKOR 90mm F4.5 f22 1/4 EPR

7 Mantokuji, "A Complete View", Edo Era (Fukui)

A great stone of a slightly more than 2.5m placed at the center of the artificial hill represents a Shumisen stone grouping. Shumisen means a high mountain towering at the heart of the world. This stone grouping was favored by garden builders in the Muromachi and Momoyama Eras. The temple is located on the bank of the Onyu River in the suburbs of Obama City. There are a number of old shrines and temples, including Jinguji, in the region.
SINAR P NIKKOR 90mm F4.5 f16 1/8 EPR

8 Former Private Garden of Mr. Sakai's, "Rock Island", Edo Era (Yamagata)

The garden, site of the residence of retired Lord Sakai, the chief of the fief of Shonai, was renovated in 1971 and opened as the garden of the Chido museum of Tsuruoka City. "Waterfall" boulders in the artificial hill, as well as the carefully maintained garden resembling the scene of a ravine, make the visitor feel refreshed. The thick greenery mirrored on the pond is beautiful.
SINAR P FUJINON 210mm F5.6 f22 1/4 EPR

9 Takidanji, "The Central Part of Chitei", Edo Era (Fukui)

Fukui Prefecture is rich with old gardens. The Takidanji Temple near Tojinbo, a well-known scenic spot, covers an area of about 1,900 m² (nineteen thousand square feet). The elongated garden with a flowing stream gains great power from the stone grouping for shore protection. The stone bridge to the sandbar behind an abbot's chamber teaches us an old technique. The plantation is well cared for and the temple has a large number of visitors during the flower season.
LINHOF KARDAN NIKKOR 90mm F4.5 f22 1/4 EPR

10 Former Umenoki Honjin, "A Complete View", Edo Era (Shiga)

This garden, located in Ritto-cho between Kusatsu and Ishibe along the old Tokaido, has artificial lakes in the eastern and western parts. An artificial hill was built in the southern part. The owner is of an old family which has dealt with the drug Wachusan for generations. The design of the garden, looking familiar and inviting while maintaining dignity, makes us feel restful.
SINAR P NIKKOR 90mm F4.5 f22 1/4 EPR

11 Former Private Garden of Mr. Yasuda's Shinshu-en, "Sawawatari Stone Grouping", Edo Era (Tokyo)

Mr. Zenjiro Yasuda largely remodelled the ruined garden of a suburban residence of the Ikeda's, the chief of the fief of Okayama. The garden, where the water of the Sumida river is introduced, is similar to the Shiba Imperial Villa and the Hama Imperial Villa in Tokyo. The features are common to these three and worth viewing. The technique of early Edo, found from place to place, is powerful enough.
SINAR P FUJINON 210mm F5.6 f22 1/4 EPR

12 Mr. Ozaki's Private Residence, "A Complete View", Edo Era (Tottori)

The 9th National Road stretches along the Sea of Japan as it comes close to Tottori. The residence of the Ozakis, an old family in the region, is in the neighborhood of Lake Togo. The green, of which Japanese sago palms are the main figures, has an exotic air. Together with the three hundred year old main building, with a saddle roof thatched with grass, the garden moves us in an inexpressible way.
LINHOF KARDAN NIKKOR 90mm F4.5 f22 1/2 EPR

13 Mr. Kakei's Private Residence, "Chitei Viewed from the Study Room", Edo Era (Hiroshima)
This was formally called Mr. Kakei's Kisui-en. The picture was taken from inside the kisui-tei pavillion, the place giving the finest view of the garden. The trees with tinted autumnal leaves are particularly beautiful. The garden is small but its technique of taking nature into it so deftly to produce a large field of vision is splendid.
SINAR P SUPERANGULON 75mm F8 f11 1/15 EPR

14 Manganji, "Stone Bridge", Edo Era (Kumamoto)
This is the most gorgeous bridge stone grouping of all the gardens covered by this photo collection. The temple in Minami-Kokunicho, at the foot of great Mt. Aso, has a long history. It was built to offer prayers for beating the enemy when the country was raided by Mongols. The atmosphere is bright, manly and full of power; the garden overwhelms us despite the small number of grand stones used.
LINHOF KARDAN FUJINON 210mm F5.6 f32 1/2 EPR

15 Mr. Noborizaka's Private Residence, "The Central Part of Karesansui", Edo Era (Iwate)
The garden in Tohno City, known for "The Tohno Story" by Kunio Yanagida, is said to have been made by a gardener invited from Kyoto, although any material to support this does not exist. With a huge Horaisan stone grouping placed at the center, it is stout and beautiful, its style befitting the former owners, the Ogasawaras, a Samurai family.
SINARP NIKKOR 90mm F4.5 f22 1/4 EPR

16 Mr. Ayugai's En-un-kan, "The Central Part of Chitei", Edo Era (Miyagi)
This is the garden of the now ruined residence of the Ayugais, the highest of the retainers of Lord Date. The garden is said to have been made during the period of Kanbun. Two Horai stone groupings are arranged on the artificial hill at the center, their stately appearance reflecting on the surface of the pond. The green background is beautiful and the whole scene is filled with a light and bright atmosphere.
SINARP NIKKOR 90mm F4.5 f22 1/4 EPR

17 Nyoshi-tei, "Sanzon Stone Grouping", Edo Era (Akita)
Akita City is a castle town which prospered for 270 years from Yoshinori Satake's founding of the Kubota Castle to the Meiji restoration. The garden is said to have been made during the Kansei period, and is presently used as a tea cottage of an inn. It has a pond as well as a dry waterfall. The general impression is rather loose but the area adjacent to this Sanzon stone grouping is gorgeous and massive.
LINHOF KARDAN FUJINON 300mm F8 f32 5 sec. EPR

18 Homma Museum, "A Complete View", Edo Era (Yamagata)
This is the garden of the Homma Museum 500m northwest of Sakata station. The Hommas are a prominent family of wealth in the Tohoku district. The garden with a pond, named Maizuru-en, was made in 1813 as a way of supporting jobless people. The view of trimmed bushes as the main feature, plus the Sawawatari (swamp path), is splendid.
LINHOF KARDAN SUPERANGULON 75mm F8 f16 1/8 EPR

19 Ryuunji, "Three-step Nagaretaki Stone Grouping", Edo Era (Niigata)
Kashiwazaki City where the temple is located is the birthplace of Sado Okesa, famous in folklore. The design of the backyard of the Study Room, making use of hillside ground and setting stone groupings of different shapes at various corners, makes us feel as if we are in a secluded place deep in the mountains. Particularly because of the three-step waterfall stone grouping high on the hillside, the garden is vigorous and full of movement.
SINAR P FUJINON 210mm F5.6 f32 2 sec. EPR

20 Gonenji, "Karetaki Stone Grouping", Edo Era (Hyogo)
The composition is powerful enough to remind us of the technique typical during the Kamakura Era. The magnificent Karetaki stone grouping in the picture is of strong appeal. An area of only about 210m² (two thousand one hundred square feet), made into a north garden of a room of the priests' living quarters, looks by no means confined owing to the garden-designer's distinguished ability.
SINAR P FUJINON 210mm F5.6 f32 1 sec. EPR

21 Yosui-en, "A Complete View", Edo Era (Wakayama)
The garden which belonged to the Tokugawa family of the fief of Kishu was called Nishihara Goten. The layout stretching from east to west is open and bright. This stroll garden has an arched bridge of Chinese type. The pond is built with a dike, and since sea water is taken in, sea fish live in the pond.
LINHOF KARDAN NIKKOR 90mm F4.5 f22 1/4 EPR

22 Unkiji, "A Complete View", Edo Era (Shimane)
Shimane abounds with old temples and shrines. This is a storied temple where Emperor Godaigo offered a prayer. In the karesansui behind the superior's quarters, trimmed azaleas are beautiful. The stone grouping for shore protection is done in a nimble, delicate way. The garden has nothing powerful but is lovely and peaceful.
MAMIYA RZ SEKOR Z 50mm F4.5 f22 1/2 EPR

23 Mr. Shoji's Private Residence, "A Complete View", Edo Era (Tottori)
The Shojis is an old family in Sakaiminato City. A well-proportioned flat stone is seen beyond the stepping stones. Visitors used to place their palanquins on it. A tea house further away has a Tachi Tsukubai (upright type wash basin) made of a natural stone. This is a typical composition of the garden in front of the Study Room. The garden is characterized by a distinctive sharpness.
LINHOF KARDAN NIKKOR 90mm F4.5 f22 1 sec. EPR

24 Mr. Sakurai's Private Residence, "Nagaretaki Stone Grouping", Edo Era (Shimane)
A waterfall cascades down a hill in the background from a height of 14m and makes a resounding sound. Lord Fumai, the chief of the fief of Matsudaira, named the waterfall "Iwanami" (rockwave). With the dignified stone grouping for shore protection, the garden is quite impressive.
LINHOF KARDAN FUJINON 210mm F5.6 f32 3 sec. EPR

25 Tensha-en, "A Complete View", Edo Era (Ehime)
It appears that the lords of the fief of Uwajima were hereditarily interested in the art of gardening. There are a number of such gardens in the city. The main feature of this garden is the area around the rock island shown in the picture. Besides the Onyoseki stone grouping and Horai stone grouping, it is also worth taking a look at the twenty kinds of bamboo grown in association with the crest of the Date family, which is another highlight.
SINAR P NIKKOR 90mm F4.5 f22 1/2 EPR

26 Mr. Naotada Sata's Private Residence, "Enzan Stone Grouping", Edo Era (Kagoshima)
Samurai residences are still left intact in Chiran-cho, Kagoshima. Each residence has its own characteristics. Among them, Mr. Sata's, surrounded by large trimmed bushes and huge stones ground to indicate a remote hill, is my favorite because it is gorgeous, powerful and straightforward.
SINAR P SUMMAR 150mm F5.6 f22 1/2 EPR

27 Enyuji, "Shudan (Mass) Stone Grouping", Edo Era (Nagasaki)
This front garden of the Study Room is composed of a large number of stone groupings. The temple itself completely perished, it gives a bit of a lonely feeling. The stone groupings resembling a dry waterfall and Sanzon (three buddhist images) fail to appeal as a whole since the technique is sharp in part but loose in other portions.
LINHOF KARDAN FUJINON 210mm F5.6 f22 1/2 EPR

28 Mr. Ie's Private Residence, "Stone Bridge of Chitei", Meiji Era (Okinawa)
It's a miracle that such a garden could escape from the flames of war at the heart of Naha City. Having an area of nearly 49,500 m² (four hundred ninety-five thousand square feet), the garden features an artificial hill and a miniature lake of orthodox Japanese style. It is a stroll garden. The photo was taken during renovation work, which has been completed beautifully.
LINHOF KARDAN SYMMAR 150mm F5.6 f22 1 sec. EPR

29 Former Zuiraku-en Garden of the Tsushima's, "A Complete View", Meiji Era (Aomori)
Gardeners who studied the art under the guidance of Teizan Takahashi, a gardener of the Bugaku school, made many fine gardens in this region. This was completed by Teizan in 1905. A waterfall stone grouping is arranged at the center and a stone bridge is laid over a dry stream. The large pine tree effectively sharpens the whole impression.
SINAR P NIKKOR 90mm F4.5 f22 1/4 EPR

30 Former Kasai-so Villa, "The Central Part of Karesansui", Meiji Era (Iwate)
This is the present backyard of the Iwate Broadcasting Station. The garden, abundant with plants and meticulously cared for, looks very clean and pure. The formation reminds us of running water. A rock island, a stone lantern and a clay bridge help present a bright and calm view despite the lack of any remarkable stone grouping. A pleasant sight.
SINAR P FUJINON 210mm F5.6 f22 1/2 EPR

31 Mr. Kon's Private Residence, "A Complete View", Meiji Era (Iwate)
The historical Tokuni Fortress built against Ezo in 813 exists in the neighborhood. In this south garden of the Study Room, eyes are first attracted to a long pond stretching from side to side. The shore protection stone grouping is stirring and full of power. Abundantly planted trees present varied views from season to season; their reflections in the pond are picturesque.
LINHOF KARDAN NIKKOR 90mm F5.6 f22 1/2 EPR

32 Mr. Koyama's Kiyo-tei, "A Complete View", Meiji Era (Yamagata)
A number of gardens made between the late Edo Era and the Meiji Era are scattered all over Sakata City, Yamagata. The designer of this garden is Soyu Yamada, a gardener of Shonai. The historical facts about the garden are clearly known. The site is 3,300 m² (thirty-three thousand square feet) in dimension. The green appears to be wrapping the whole garden, and inside a rock island, a sandbar, a zigzag bridge and pond breath quietly. Deep serenity prevails.
LINHOF KARDAN NIKKOR 90mm F5.6 f22 1 sec. EPR

33 Hoppo Bunka Museum, "A Complete View", Meiji Era (Niigata)
The garden of the museum was founded based on a donation from Mr. Bunkichi Ito, a large land owner of the district. The place, along the Agano River, is famous for its scenic beauty. The general impression resembles the garden of a ceremonial teahouse. Two stone bridges are built over the pond to the rock island. The stepping stones are widely spaced and have a light, cheerful air.
SINAR P NIKKOR 90mm F4.5 f22 1/2 EPR

34 Mr. Senke's Private Residence, "A Complete View", Meiji Era (Shimane)
The Sen family has served God as the governors of Izumo for generations. The north garden of the inner Study Room fully becomes the class of the family. The red gravel of the Iinashi River spread over the garden presents a graceful beauty. The rectangular pavement stones and the stepping stones are the main features of it.
SINAR P NIKKOR 90mm F4.5 f22 1/2 EPR

35 Former Sakyoya Mr. Matsuura's Private Residence, "The Central Part of Chitei", Meiji Era (Shiga)
Santo-cho Kashiwabara at the foot of Mt. Ibuki is a post town of the old Nakasendo. The residence with a stylish gate is owned by Mr. Matsuura, a long-established trader of Ibuki moxa. The garden and its reflection on the water viewed from a room are beautiful. The tidy appearance, with nothing ostentatious about it, is likable.
SINAR P SYMMAR 150 mm F5.6 f22 1/2 EPR

36 Murin-an, "Stream in the Central Part of the Garden", Meiji Era (Kyoto)
This is a masterpiece of Jihei Ogawa, a reputed gardener known as Ueji of Kyoto. Aritomo Yamagata, a veteran statesman of the Imperial Restoration of Meiji, had it made. The garden, with a stream of water taken in from the Kamo River, uses Higashi-yama Hills as its borrowed background. A harmony of refined artificial beauty and natural beauty, it varies in appearance as the seasons advance and keeps fascinating us.
SINAR P FUJINON 210 mm F5.6 f22 1/2 EPR

37 Isui-en, "Sawawatari Stepping Stones", Meiji Era (Nara)
Sawawatari stepping stones similar to these are found in the Heian Shrine. By making use of old stone mortars, a rare scene is created. Alternate arrangements have the same function as a zigzag bridge, to provide a different field of vision at every step.
SINAR P FUJINON 300 mm F8 f22 1/2 EPR

38 Isui-en, "The Snowy Chitei", Meiji Era (Nara)
This grand spectacle with the South Gate of Todaiji is full of dynamism. The garden belonged to Mr. Jiro Sekito, who made a fortune in the staple fiber business, but is presently taken care of by the Nara Museum. The front garden was made in the Edo Era and the back garden shown in this photograph was made in the Meiji Era. One of the best of the period.
SINAR P NIKKOR 90 mm F4.5 f22 1 sec. EPR

39 Mr. Tachibana's Shoto-en Garden, "The Central Part of Chitei", Meiji Era (Fukuoka)
The garden is located in Yanagawa, the hometown of famous poet Hakushu Kitahara. The Shoto-en villa was built by Akitora Tachibana, the fourth liege lord, and largely remodeled during the Meiji Era. Now it is the main attraction for sightseers of Yanagawa. Nearly one hundred rock islands and more than two hundred fifty old pine trees are particularly beautiful.
LINHOF KARDAN FUJINON 210 mm F5.6 f22 1/2 EPR

40 Mr. Furukawa's Private Residence
"A Complete View of Karikomi", Taisho Era (Tokyo)
The place was once the private residence of Mr. Ichibei Furukawa, a tycoon of the mining industry. British architect Condle designed this garden. He cleverly took advantage of the sloped ground. The beauty expressed by the straight and curved lines of trimmed bushes displays the characteristics of the European-style garden. The garden in the lower part was made by Ueji, a gardener of Kyoto. It is worth visiting.
MAMIYA RZ SEKOR 50 mm F4.5 f16 1/8 EPR

41 Mr. Hashimoto's Hakusha-sonso, "Stone Buddhist Images in a Bamboo Forest", Taisho Era (Kyoto)
This is the atelier and residence of Kansetsu Hashimoto, a painter of traditional Japanese style, who played an active role in this field between Taisho and early Showa. Various stone objects set in the garden eloquently tell how the artist loved stones. The Buddhist images quietly sitting in the bamboo forest are delightful and make us smile.
MAMIYA RZ SEKOR 90mm F3.8 f22 1/2 EPR

42 Mr. Hashimoto's Hakusha-sonso, "Seven-story Pagoda", Taisho Era (Kyoto)
The time was deeply tinted with the naturalistic trend of thought and bringing stone articles into private gardens was in fashion. At the same time, the study of stone objects thrived. A multi-story pagoda connotes an offering for the repose of the soul of the dead or a stupa but those in this garden are rather an element of the scene.
MAMIYA RZ SEKOR 90 mm F3.8 f22 1/2 EPR

43 Mr. Hashimoto's Hakusha-sonso, "Hokyoin Pagoda", Taisho Era (Kyoto)
The Hokyoin Pagoda originated in India, has an angular shape, a square when viewed from above. Usually, Kohazama is carved on the surfaces of the base and Sanskrit characters are carved on the body of the Hokyoin Pagoda for use as a tower erected for the repose of the soul of the dead or a grave stone. The one in this photo is superb. The shape is fine. It has an inscrption from the second year of Eitoku.
MAMIYA RZ SEKOR 180 mm F5.6 f22 1/2 EPR

44 Mr. Hashimoto's Hakusha-sonso, "Kunisaki Sekido", Taisho Era (Kyoto)
The Kunisaki Peninsula of Kyushu abounds with stone Buddhist images and stone monuments. Their researchers do not fail to visit there. Sekido shown here is characteristic of the region and so is called by this name. The stone is cut into a hexagon and each surface is carved into a Buddhist image. It is also called Rokumendo.
MAMIYA RZ SEKOR 180 mm F5.6 f22 1/2 EPR

45 Mr. Hashimoto's Hakusha-sonso, "Stone Buddhist Relief", Taisho Era (Kyoto)
Sculptured images of Buddha on rock walls of hills or natural stone walls are frequently seen in India and China. Here in Japan, such reliefs abound in Kunisaki, Nara and Ohmi and are scattered throughout some other regions. The relief in this garden is an image of Jizo. The innocent expression is very charming.
MAMIYA RZ SEKOR 90 mm F3.8 f16 1/8 EPR

46 Sankei-en, "A Complete View", Taisho Era (Kanagawa)
This was the principal residence of Tomitaro Hara, a wealthy merchant of silk and an art lover. The garden is richly endowed by nature with its fine components of hills, ponds and dales. It offers enjoyment during every season. About all the scenery which includes cultural assets transferred from various places and arranged at appropriate spots, is overwhelmingly beautiful.
LINHOF KARDAN NIKKOR 90 mm F4.5 f22 1/2 EPR

47 Sankei-en, "Shunsoro", Taisho Era (Kanagawa)
Tomitaro Hara who had the nom de plume of Sankei loved the tea cult. Shunsoro which was transferred from Konzo-in in Uji is a Sanjodaime (a ceremonial tearoom with three-mat space for guests) and is said to be of Oda Urakusai style. The path leading to it is laid with stirring Garan (cathedral) stones. Stepping stones are informally placed and the rustic scene is pleasantly simple and quiet.
LINHOF KARDAN SYMMAR 150 mm F5.6 f22 1 sec. EPR

48 Sankei-en, "Shunsoro Tsukubai", Taisho Era (Kanagawa)
A Shihobutsu water basin, constructed from a Hokyoin Pagoda and a multi-story pagoda, is placed at the center and the surrounding green is kept appropriately simple. The scene is tasteful, well matched to the simple, hermitage-tyle garden. The Yotsume-gaki (four-eyed fence) in the back is perfect as an element in the picture.
LINHOF KARDAN SYMMAR 150 mm F5.6 f22 1 sec. EPR

49 Roka Sensui-so, "Flagstones", Taisho Era(Shiga)
This was built as the villa of Shunkyo Yamamoto, a Japanese-style painter. Formerly the shore of Lake Biwa was closer and provided a beautiful background landscape. The view underwent a drastic change when the coastal road was built. The line of flagstones leading to the door audaciously turns to the right, depicting a beautiful and dynamic curve.
SINAR FUJINON 210mm F5.6 f32 1 sec. EPR

50 Roka Sensui-so, "Lantern", Taisho Era(Shiga)
The stone lantern is placed on the side of the water basin shown in the following picture. The rod portion is buried under ground. Usually, there should be a base stone below the rod but the technique is often used for the tea garden or the path to the tearoom. A creative idea attaching importance to the practical side of the object.
SINAR P SUPERANGULON 75mm F8 f22 1 sec. EPR

51 Roka Sensui-so, "Water Basin", Taisho Era (Shiga)
The water basin called Chozubachi of Hashirii is made of a stone mortar used to pound glutinous rice for making Hashirii Mochi (ricecake) at a tea stall in Osakayama. The functional quality of the utensil becomes a beautiful design. The inversed reflection on the surface of the water filling the basin presents a refreshing appearance.
MAMIYA RZ SEKOR 90 mm F3.8 f22 1/2 EPR

52 Heian Shrine, "Sawawatari Stepping Stones", Taisho Era (Kyoto)
The Heian Shrine, built in 1895 on the occasion of the one thousand one hundredth anniversary of the transfer of the capital to Kyoto, is full of tourists. The Sawawatari stones in the picture are old pillars of the Great Bridge of Sanjo. It is interesting to note that this makes an excellent contrast with the Sawawatari of Isui-en, Nara.
LINHOF KARDAN FUJINON 210 mm F5.6 f32 1 sec. EPR

53 Heian Shrine, "Pavilion over a Pond", Taisho Era (Kyoto)
This is a work of Jihei Ogawa, alias Ueji, who was the most active gardener at the time. He began making the East Garden of the Shrine, in which this pavilion was built, in 1914. The pavilion designed so as to traverse the pond, with Higashiyama Hills as the background, reflects its elegant form in the pond. The green is attractive in all the seasons and is particularly beautiful in spring, adorned with cherry blossoms.
LINHOF KARDAN FUJINON 300 mm F8 f22 1/2 EPR

54 Onzan-so, "Garden Path and Chitei", Taisho Era (Wakayama)
This is a vast Chitei covering an area of 99,000 m² (nine hundred ninety-nine thousand square feet). Another garden resembling this, Yosui-en, is also located in the city. This is a typical stroll garden, and the pond is fed by sea water. A number of rock islands in the pond make this a beautiful scene, and people in the city love to stroll here.
LINHOF KARDAN NIKKOR 90 mm F5.6 f22 1/2 EPR

55 Komyozen-in, "Moss", Present Age (Kyoto)
The beauty of the moss is something special among the components of the garden. Hair cap moss is difficult to grow here. Watering every morning and evening is indispensable. Its soft touch is pleasing and its green color is most impressive. Moss is used in many dry landscape gardens.
MAMIYA RZ SEKOR 90 mm F3.8 f22 1/2 EPR

56 Mr. Shigemori's Private Residence, "Ajiromon", Present Age (Kyoto)
White pebbles and green moss are indispensable elements in the dry landscape garden. They express a vast ocean, a great river or a current. Ajiro are braided bamboo or wooden sticks used instead of a net for fishing, in rapids. The designs of lattice are also called Ajiro.
MAMIYA RZ SEKOR 90 mm F3.8 f22 1/4 EPR

57 Mr. Shigemori's Private Residence, "Igetamon", Present Age (Kyoto)
From what time such patterns were depicted with white pebbles is not known. Designs of sand patterns or patterns drawn with a broom express extreme cleanliness. The idea is peculiar to Japan. Igetamon is designed out of a Kana character resembling parallel crosses.
MAMIYA RZ SEKOR 90 mm F3.8 f22 1/4 EPR

58 Mr. Shigemori's Private Residence, "Seikaihamon", Present Age (Kyoto)
This is the pattern of the costume of Seikaiha, a court music piece. It was popular around the time of Genroku. We often see the pattern in the scale portion on a carp flag. The design spreading toward the end suggests a vast expanse of ocean and serves to make a limited space look wide.
MAMIYA RZ SEKOR 90 mm F3.8 f22 1/4 EPR

59 Mr. Shigemori's Private Residence, "Uzumakimon", Present Age (Kyoto)
Uzumaki means a design of volute which reminds us of the eddying current of Naruto or a mosquito-repellent incense. This is probably the pattern most frequently used in dry landscape gardens. Particularly, it is adopted in gardens which have Funaishi (stones symbolizing a ship). The expression of dynamic currents is powerful.
MAMIYA RZ SEKOR 90 mm F3.8 f22 1/4 EPR

60 Mr. Shigemori's Private Residence, "Ajiromon Variation", "Present Age (Kyoto)
A virtue of the sand pattern is that one can give form to one's idea without restriction. Some garden-lovers are said to enjoy the hard labor of drawing sand patterns every morning and evening with tools they have invented themselves. Dry landscape gardens are easy to take care of. That is why they are popular these days.
MAMIYA RZ SEKOR 90 mm F3.8 f22 1/4 EPR

61 Mr. Shigemori's Private Residence, "Kyokusenmon", Present Age (Kyoto)
All the sand patterns shown here were drawn by me using Mr. Shigemori's garden as a canvas. I hope they will give a general idea of sand patterns. Who invented such a technique? Wonderful wisdom that grew over a long period is evident.
MAMIYA RZ SEKOR 90 mm F3.5 f22 1/4 EPR

62 Matsuo Taisha, "Iwakura (Egoishi Stone Grouping)", Present Age (Kyoto)
My teacher, Mirei Shigemori, created Iwakura and Iwasaka at three places. The huge stone at the center is erected so as to face Iwakura on the hilltop. It is called Egoishi. The master's pure spirit aspiring to be closer to God was sublimated with this last work of his and his soul went to God. For me, this will be an unforgettable garden as long as I live.
SINAR P FUJINON 210 mm F5.6 f32 1/2 EPR

63 Tofukuji, "The Central Part of Karesansui", Present Age (Kyoto)
Four gardens are positioned so as to enclose the living quarters of the chief priest. All of them were made by Mirei Shigemori. The garden with only flat stones and moss is called the garden of Ichimatsu (checks). It was completed in 1938. The modernity based on tradition is rated high.
LINHOF KARDAN FUJINON 210 mm F5.6 f32 1 sec. EPR

64 Tofukuji, "A Partial View of Karesansui", Present Age (Kyoto)
This is the front garden of the priest's quarters viewed from a connecting corridor. Stones selected very carefully are grouped exquisitely to produce a neat and clean but exciting atmosphere suitable for a Zen temple. The standing figure of a huge stone, looking as if it had grown out of the earth, strikes us with an indescribable sensation. A masterpiece of gardens of the present age. My teacher's youthful, energetic passion is crystalized in it.
LINHOF KARDAN NIKKOR 90 mm F5.6 f22 1/2 EPR

65 Tofukuji, "A Complete View", Present Age (Kyoto)
This is the front garden of the priest's quarters, called the garden of Horai. The stone groupings are Horai, Hoji, Eishu and Koryo, named after the miracle islands of perennial youth that appear in Chinese legends. They bring images of islands in the sea to one's mind, and a very tense feeling grips one.
LINHOF KARDAN NIKKOR 90 mm F4.5 f22 1/2 EPR

66 Shokakuji, "A Complete View" Present Age (Hyogo)
A Taki stone grouping of the Ryumonbaku style is seen on the right side in the central part. A Rigyo stone, suggesting carp, is trying to ascend to heaven. Three bridges made of Aoishi (blue stone) connect Tsurushima (Crane Island) and Kameshima (Tortoise Island). This is a good garden to study for the composition is based on a thorough knowledge of classic garden design.
LINHOF KARDAN SUPERANGULON 75 mm F8 f22 1 sec. EPR

67 Kozenji, "A Complete View", Present Age (Nagano)
This garden, which is similar to that of Shokakuji above, was made by Mirei Shigemori. Although the common practice is to liken white pebbles to the sea, a river or a current, these were intended to represent a sea of clouds, he said. Accordingly, the stone groupings are high peaks above a sea of clouds, with other details left to the interpretation of the viewers.
SINAR P SUPRFANGULON 75 mm F8 f22 1/4 EPR

68 Shogunzuka, "Around the Stone Bridge", Present Age (Kyoto)
Shogunzuka is a mound in which a statue of a warlord was buried to face the west, so as to pray for peace for the imperial capital. The stone bridge is laid low and Bunsuiseki, a water-shedding stone of impressive form, is set. This garden was made by Kinsaku Nakane, who has the most complete mastery of the classic garden-designing art among the experts of our age. The Kyoto Jonangu is his masterpiece.
SINAR P FUJINON 210 mm F5.6 f22 1/2 EPR

69 Adachi Art Museum, "The Central Part of Karesansui", Present Age (Shimane)
The principal collection of the museum is modern Japanese-style paintings. The animating stone grouping is powerful and large in scale, making use of Katsuyama and Gassan as a background. The scene includes low pine trees and deserves to be called masterpiece of the present age. The above Shogunzuka of the classic style and this garden of his original design both show the high standard of Mr. Nakane's skill.
SINAR SYMMAR 150 mm F5.6 f2 1/2 EPR

70 Komine Shrine, "Flagstones", Present Age (Tochigi)
Flagstones of Hosho-an is a tea arbor built at one corner of the spacious precincts. Surrounded with thick moss, they invite visitors into the grove along a gentle curve. It was designed by Mr. Kotaro Iwaki, a great master of garden-designing in our age. He is a nephew of Jihei Ogawa, a gardener genius of the Meiji Era, and was trained by his uncle.
SINAR P FUJINON 210 mm F5.6 f32 2 sec. EPR

71 Komine Shrine, "Nagaretaki Stone Grouping", Present Age (Tochigi)
One reaches this garden across a natural grove. This is the thirteen meter head of a voluminous water fall to one artificial lake 3,950 m² (thirty-nine thousand five hundred square feet) wide. Mr. Iwaki's style is delicate and elaborate. He designed many gardens abroad. Modern Japanese landscape gardening art owes much to him.
SINAR P FUJINON 210 mm F5.6 f32 1 sec. EPR

72 Ryugen-in, "A Complete View of the East Garden", Present Age (Kyoto)
Ryugen-in, a temple affiliated with Daitokuji, Kyoto, has a long history and its Hojo, the living quarters of the priest, is the oldest building of its kind of the Muromachi Era. A limited space of only about thirteen square meters is found in the East Garden leading to the Hojo. The space is called Totekitsubo. It's nothing but five stones arranged vertically but causes a very tense feeling, probably because of the designer's caliber. A strange garden, indeed.
SINAR P SUPERANGLON 75 mm F8 f22 1 sec. EPR

73 Mr. Morita's Private Residence, "A View from a Room", Present Age (Chiba)
Boulders are arranged in a limited space. With the stone bridge laid low and the Sanzon stone grouping in front, the garden is full of movement almost bursting. The designer is Mr. Mirei Shigemori's son, Kanto. He wrote many books and designed a number of gardens, introducing Japanese gardening to the world.
SINAR P SYMMAR 150 mm F5.6 f32 1 sec. EPR

74 Mr. Yano's Private Residence, "A View from the Study Room", Present Age (Tokushima)
The garden was made on a rectangular lot, with a deep mountain dwelled on by God as its theme. It's about 99 m² (nine hundred and ninety square feet) in area. The slant stone grouping is of Muromachi style. Carefully chosen stones shine. The designer is the foremost pupil of Mirei Shigemori. He calls himself Ishidateso (stone erecting monk). He is well versed in the tea cult.
SINAR P SYMMAR 150 mm F5.6 f32 1/2 EPR

75 Hotel Koyokan, "The Central Part of Chitei", Present Age (Iwate)
A rectangular space in front of the lobby was enclosed by an earthen wall and the Chitei was made there. The combination of white pebbles and Chitei is a bold stroke. The concept of mixing classic techniques and original portions produces a gentle, naturalistic landscape. Mr. Ken Nakajima, the designer, studied old gardens and currently designs colorful gardens.
SINAR P FUJINON 210 mm F5.6 f32 1 sec. EPR

76 Hotel Hanamaki, "Nagaretaki Stone Grouping", Present Age (Iwate)
Hanamaki Hot Spring was developed in 1923 by piping hot water from the Dai hot spring. The bright and healthy town has beautiful rows of cherry and pine trees. Gardens are often planted in hotels and inns. The taki stone grouping is conservative, naturalistic and heart-warming.
SINAR P FUJINON 210 mm F5.6 f32 1 sec. EPR

77 Hotel Hanamaki, "Otsu-gaki Variation", Present Age (Iwate)
The hedge belongs to the above garden. Bamboo were split into flat sticks and braided by arranging them alternately with surface and back side out into patterns of the Ajiro style. The plain fence matches the composition indicating a seashore landscape. The technique of making full use of the fence while also using it as a design element in the scene shows matured skill and is most effective.
SINAR P SYMMAR 150 mm F5.6 f22 2 sec. EPR

78 Kifune-cho, "Chasen-gaki", Present Age (Kyoto)
The fence is an original creation shaped like the bamboo whisk used for making ceremonial tea. It is frequently used for tea houses and inns. It has nothing suggesting inaccessibility. The naiive, lovely design is favored by masters and students of the tea cult.
MAMIYA RZ SEKOR 90 mm F3.8 f16 1/4 EPR

79 Tokoen Hotel, "Daitokuji-gaki", Present Age (Tottori)
The original was in the precincts of Daitokuji, Kyoto, and hence, it has this name. Sprigs of bamboo are put together, arranged from right to left and stuck in the ground. Then, hemp palm rope is used to tie them in a cross shape. These are often found around middle gates or middle wicket gates of rustic cottages and gardens of tea arbors.
LINHOF KARDAN SYMMAR 150 mm F5.6 f16 1/8 EPR

80 Kifune-cho, "Katsura-gaki Variation", Present Age (Kyoto)
The original Katsura-gaki is the bamboo fence on the left side of the Katsura Imperial Villa entrance. Between log bamboo, joint material is pierced and ears of small bamboo are inserted. There are numerous imitations of this bamboo fence but none are comparable to the original.
MAMIYA SEKOR 90 mm F3.8 f16 1/15 EPR

81 Hanamaki Hot Spring, "Sosaku-gaki", Present Age (Iwate)
Landscape gardeners create new fences according to uses. Unlike board fences which completely interrupt views, fences placed inside a garden should not mar appearances around it. That is the difficult part of creating but I expect a lot from it.
LINHOF KARDAN SYMMAR 150 mm F5.6 f22 1/2 EPR

82 Mr. Idemitsu's Private Residence, "The Middle Gate of Choseki-an", Present Age (Tokyo)
This is the garden adjacent to Choseki-an and it is a copy of the thatched gate of Omote Senke. The middle gate is where the host receives his guest. They exchange greetings on both sides of the gate. It is an important place as the guest meets the host for the first time there. The dusted and watered area is beautiful.
SINAR P NIKKOR 90 mm F4.6 f22 1 sec. EPR

83 Mr. Idemitsu's Private Residence, "Yakuishi at the Middle Gate of Choseki-an", Present Age (Tokyo)
The mid-wicket gate of the middle gate is opened. The large stone in the foreground is Yakuishi, guest's stone. The lower one is teishuishi, host's stone. Both are indispensable at the middle gate of the tea garden. Along the path from the cleaned gate area to the tea arbor, the scene presented is of a field with undergrowth planted low.
SINAR P SUPERANGULON 75 mm F8 f22 1 sec. EPR

84 Mr. Okazaki's Private Residence, "Seisui-an Nakakuguri (Wicket Gate)", Present Age (Fukuoka)
This is the middle wicket gate of the garden adjacent to Seisui-an. The gate separates the inner garden and the outer garden. It is said that such a gate did not exist at the time of Rikyu. The middle wicket gate of Omote-senke is a work of the early period of the tea cult. The area around this wicket gate is sonorously made in the Kyoto style. The slightly opened door means that a guest is inside.
LINHOF KARDAN SYMMAR 150 mm F5.6 f22 2 sec. EPR

85 Mr. Okazaki's Private Residence, "Seisui-an Tsukubai", Present Age (Fukuoka)

A water basin made of a splendid corner stone is placed in front of the Seisui-an tea arbor. The basin is low since hands are washed in a crouching style. Tsukubai is always necessary for the garden adjacent to a tea-ceremony room because guests purify themselves mentally and physically by using it before participating in the tea ceremony.
LINHOF KARDAN FUJINON 210 mm F5.6 f32 2 sec. EPR

86 Hakone Art Museum, "Around the Sangetsu-an", Present Age (Kanagawa)

The tea ceremony house standing in the garden of the museum, above Gora Park, was built by old Mr. Mokichi Okada, the founder of the Sekai Kyusei-Kai. Because of the cold winter here, frost affects stepping stones and moss adversely. In this view the winter protection which covers them with straw is particularly tasteful.
SINAR P SYMMAR 150 mm F5.6 f22 1/2 EPR

87 Hakone Art Museum, "The Middle Gate of Sangetsu-an", Present Age (Kanagawa)

Finely shaped flagstones lead to the middle gate. While stepping stones are arranged in accordance with strides so that each stone can come under each foot, flagstones are laid widely without spaces between them. The latter is rather monotonous but safe and easy to walk on. The skill of the garden designer is fully demonstrated in the handling of both stepping stones and flagstones.
SINAR P NIKKOR 90 mm F4.5 f16 1/2 EPR

88 Hakone Art Museum, "Sangetsu-an Machiai", Present Age (Kanagawa)

This is Machiai (a waiting place) of Sangetsu-an. A rustic feeling prevails in the subdued, cottage-style structure. Originally, Sotokoshikake (outside bench) was called Machiai and Uchikoshikake (inside bench) was called Koshikake but now they are together called Koshikake-machiai. The tea ceremony house had only one Machiai formerly but the number increased as the double and triple gardens were developed.
SINAR P NIKKOR 90 mm F4.5 f22 1 sec. EPR

89 Tea Ceremony Association (Dainihon Chado Gakkai), "Santoku-an Nijiriguchi", Present Age (Tokyo)

The association was founded by old Mr. Sensho Tanaka. He aims at rational Chanoyu, on the theory that no school is necessary for the tea cult. Rikyu, who called the garden adjacent to a tea arbor 'Roji' (literal translation is revealed ground) taught that the name meant revealing the merciful heart by getting rid of irrelevant thoughts.
LINHOF KARDAN SYMMAR 150 mm F5.6 f22 1/2 EPR

90 Tea Ceremony Association (Dainihon Chado Gakkai), "Santoku-an Machiai", Present Age (Tokyo)

Machiai is also called Yoritsuki or Hakamatsuki. There are no restrictions on style or location. A room in the living quarters may be used. This Machiai of Santoku-an, sprinkled with water and filled with the sense of purity, is equipped with a tobacco tray and round straw mats and has the restrained feeling peculiar to the garden of a tea arbor. Very refreshing.
LINHOF KARDAN SYMMAR 150 mm F5.6 f22 1/2 EPR

91 Tea Ceremony Association (Dainihon Chado Gakkai), "Santoku-an Chiriana", Present Age (Tokyo)

This is the pit into which fallen leaves and refuse are dumped. It is customary to provide one near the Nijiriguchi of a tea ceremony room. Most of these pits are round or square. As a rule, a pair of green bamboo chopsticks is furnished. The chopsticks are also called Chiriana Kazari (dust hole ornament). Simple beauty is characteristic of the garden adjacent to a ceremonial tea house.
LINHOF KARDAN SYMMAR 150 mm F5.6 f22 2 sec. EPR

92 Tea Ceremony Association (Dainihon Chado Gakkai), "The Well of Santoku-an", Present Age (Tokyo)

The well indispensable to the tea ceremony is Ido or Izutsu in Japanese. The form of stones arranged into double crosses is animating and powerful. About the well, pine needles are spread to protect stepping stones and moss. At the Hakone Art Museum leaves are used for the same purpose.
LINHOF KARDAN SYMMAR 150 mm F5.6 f22 2 sec. EPR

AFTERWORD

In Japan today there are approximately 1300 Japanese gardens. They are gardens that have a history from ancient times and are still admired and enjoyed. If modern-day gardens (temples and shrines, parks, government and municipal buildings, art museums, hotel, private residences, etc.) were included, the number would exceed 10,000. I have introduced about 200 gardens up to now combining the ones included in this book along with those in my last collection "Japanese Garden". Although only 10 percent were shown, I would be pleased beyond expectation if readers find full spiritual enjoyment in the beauty of Japanese gardens.

Master Mirei Shigemori taught me to highly regard stone grouping. Once he and I went on a photographing expedition. We happened to photograph a temple garden. That garden had so many plantain lilies that they hid the Gogan stone grouping. At first sight it seemed to be a beautiful garden with all the glorious flowers. He spoke a word or two with the head priest. Then he took a sickle in his hand and he promptly started cutting down the plantain lilies, when at once a stirring bold stone grouping appeared. Completely different from its previous state the vastness of the garden opened up before my eyes.

At that instant it evoked the conversation about the morning glory between Hideyoshi and Rikyu at tea party. Although differing in meaning, it had the same essence in my heart. I was deeply moved at Master Shigemori's devotion to gardens and his strict attitude towards stone grouping. Since that time, it would not be exaggerating to say my pictures of gardens do not contain flowers. Beautiful scenes of flowers are fewer in this latest collection of mine (Japanese Gardens of the Modern Era) and I hope you will understand it.

This book is a collection of gardens including the ancient Iwakura Gardens, the origin of Japanese gardens, along with gardens from the end of the Edo period to modern-day. As readers will notice, a distinguishing point through this process extending to modern-day with the exception of the Edo period is that gardens shown from Meiji onward are almost all privately owned (although privately owned, they include old daimyos and family estates). One may wonder why there are practically no temple gardens. I am not a historian or a scholar on Japanese gardens. I have only taken a number of pictures of gardens and have seen and heard more than the common person. I guess it is due to the following two reasons.

The first is that in the first year of Meiji an edict on the separation of Shintoism and Buddhism was enacted. The anti-Buddhist movement was circulating nationwide. Temples were destroyed. Buddhist images, paintings, scriptures, etc. were burned. Amidst the confrontation of the supporting and opposing groups the temples probably did not have the energy economically or spiritually to construct gardens. A second view is due to the Sino-Japanese and the Russo-Japanese Wars. They probably did not have the financial means to construct gardens even if they wanted.

Whatever the case, there were very few temple gardens built from Meiji to present day which is a notable phenomenon.

This situation continued until 1928 when Mirei Shigemori constructed a garden for the head priest of Tofukuji Temple. It was built by service without remuneration. This garden embodied the passion of his youth. The complicated intricate construction of both old and new gardens have won high acclaim. Temple gardening construction which had been asleep suddenly became ignited. Mr. Shigemori's achievements are great, and of even greater significance in helping to develop the modern day garden.

It is not my place as an amateur to say how gardens will be transformed in the future or how what place they will have in Japanese society; however, in one word, modern gardens are difficult to understand. I myself prefer old-style gardens. I am filled with anxiety as to how the readers will react to this book.

In closing I would like to express my appreciation to Asako Muroo who wrote the foreword and Kakuzo Akahira of Graphic-Sha Publishing Co., Ltd., who was a great service once again in the planning and progress of the book with words of advice. Also, I would like to thank designer Hiroto Kumagai and Koen Shigemori who carefully studied my photographs. Last of all, I wish that Master Mirei Shigemori could see this. May he rest in peace.

July, 1986

Haruzo Ohashi